AROUND MY GARDEN
80 IN YEARS

Jon Cunningham's *Around My Garden in Eighty Years* is a wonderful read, not only for master gardeners but all levels of growers. It is well-written and illustrated providing both humor and tips based on a lifetime of growing sustainable fruits, vegetables and succulents. The author's depth of knowledge is obvious by his gifted discussions of soils, water, seeds, and contemporary techniques.

~A. LEE BROWN JR., PH.D.
Professor *emeritus*
Author of *The Varsity, A Story of America's Underage Warriors in WWII*

Jon Cunningham's love of gardening shines through in this very practical and information-packed book. This is a must read for the aspiring gardener.

~LAWRENCE MULRYAN
Master Gardener
Former Mayor of San Raphael, California
Former CEO of California State Workman's Compensation Fund

AROUND
MY GARDEN
80 IN YEARS

AROUND MY GARDEN
80 IN YEARS

My Adventure with Soil, Sun and Water

SUSTAINABILITY, EASY COMPOSTING, IMMUNE BOOSTERS, HEALTH AND LONGEVITY, VEGETABLE AND FRUIT SELF SUFFICIENCY, CREATIVE GRAFTING (FUN AND EASY), CONTAINER GARDENING

DR. JON CUNNINGHAM

For information about this title, contact the publisher:

4Paws Press
www.digdiego.com
jjsierra1937@gmail.com

ISBNs:
978-1-7369282-0-2 (softcover)
978-1-7369282-1-9 (eBook)

Printed in the United States of America

Cover and Interior design: 1106 Design

Disclaimer
The information in this book is true and complete to the best of my knowledge. All recommendations are made without guarantee on the part of the author.

This book is dedicated to my lovely wife Joan,
whose sunny personality makes her so nice to be around.
Her devotion and support are unending . . .
how lucky can a guy get?

Contents

Introduction

I grew up in San Diego, in a community called Loma Portal. As a boy, I had plenty to keep me busy on any given Saturday, with a long list of chores, which typically included mowing the lawn and lots of weeding. If I had finished all my chores when my dad came home from his dental office, he would take me in his box trailer down to pick up horse manure in Mission Valley. We would load up the box trailer with the manure, and I would get to ride on top of the pile all the way home. This was my big thrill for the week as, back then, we didn't have TVs or computers. I also kept busy with my many pets, including my pet raccoon (in those days, you could buy raccoons and de-scented skunks in pet stores).

My parents gardened for 52 years on a large lot behind their house. My mom, originally a farm girl from the Midwest, spent her days picking the fruits and vegetables they grew, canning much of it, making pickles, jam, and homemade pies. Between the three of us, over the years, we produced enough fruits and vegetables to easily feed ourselves, with plenty left over for friends and neighbors. Everything was organic, and no pesticides were used. This was my first gardening experience and officially when the seed was planted for my future passion.

Years later, after marrying my high-school sweetheart, finishing dental school, and starting a family, my wife and I built a house on the same block on which I grew up. We did not have quite the garden space my parents had, but we still grew everything under the sun. My dad loved coming over and giving us free advice. Our composting had "advanced" to the level of burying kitchen scraps, and fish and abalone guts in trenches and around trees, and covering it up with soil. In a couple months, it was one with the soil. This went on for 42 years, until we sold the house and moved about a mile farther south to a community called Point Loma Heights.

Our "new" 60-year-old house is 1500 square feet and perfect for empty nesters with a scruffy dog and 20-year-old cat. One great feature

My pet raccoon

of our property is that it has a nice-sized yard, in which we built five concrete-block raised gardens. We were the beneficiaries of three huge, mature fruit trees, including a Satsuma seedless tangerine, Eureka lemon, and fig.

This book is inspired by my 65-plus years of gardening and an incident that happened at my local nursery. I was there to buy some of my favorite potting soil and corn seeds, but they were sold out of both. This was the first time I had ever run into this problem. When I asked the salesperson what was going on, his response was that because of COVID-19, so many people became concerned about the food supply that they started planting Victory Gardens at home. I thought I had better get with the program, and, for the first time in my life, I started making my own above-ground compost. While I enjoyed most of the process, I definitely did not like the heavy lifting and turning of the pile. So, I started researching electric composters on the Internet and found a man demonstrating a device for turning compost called a Power Planter. It looked awesome, so I called the company and spoke with the owner, Greg Niewold. We chatted for a while, and he sent me the exact model that I needed. So, this is where the introduction ends, and the story begins . . . with chapters on the Power Planter and composting. I hope you enjoy reading it and that it helps you become the gardener you aspire to be.

CHAPTER 1

Sustainability

There are many definitions of "sustainability," but the one I like best and for purposes of this book is: "The avoidance of the depletion of natural resources in order to maintain balance. In the 21st century, it refers generally to the capacity for the biosphere and human civilization to coexist." In terms of backyard gardening, sustainability is the ability to maintain the soil integrity, quality of fruits and vegetables produced, and pest management with only positive impact. When you are reading this book, you will see that I still have a way to go before I reach the level of sustainability I desire.

My friend and neighbor of forty years, John, came to the United States from Portugal in 1960. He brought with him seeds from fava beans and tomatoes and cuttings from a fig and cherimoya tree. Fava beans are a large variety popular in Portugal and other Mediterranean countries. Cherimoyas, my favorite fruit, are about the size and shape of an average artichoke and taste like a combination of banana, mango, and papaya. I drove by his house many times and admired his figs, which were big and purple, and almost the size of a tennis ball. I had previously eaten cherimoyas and wanted to try growing them in my yard. One day around 1980, John was out in his garden, and I stopped by, introduced myself, and asked him where he bought his fig and cherimoya trees. Like all gardeners, he was happy to have somebody admiring his garden and offered me a fig. I already had three fig trees at home producing way more than we could ever eat, but my theory was one can never have too many figs, especially when you have lots of neighbors with Portuguese or Italian backgrounds. Another neighbor, originally from Mexico, had two small poodles that absolutely love figs, too. When I bit into John's fig, the inside reminded me of delicious strawberry jam—it was nothing like any fig I'd ever tasted. Long story short, I ended up with a fig-tree cutting and one from his cherimoya tree (this will be continued in the chapters on figs, grafting, and cherimoyas). I followed John, stopping by his garden quite often, and tried to learn as much as I could. His technique was about as sustainable as you could find and very simple and straightforward. For 60 years now, he has gardened the same way, in which he plants two successive crops of fava beans starting in November. Usually, he has about 10 rows about twenty feet long each. He lets the last two rows go to seed, as will be explained in the chapter on fava beans. He composts his large (about five feet tall) beanstalks usually around April or May and lets the ground take a rest for a month or so. Part of the fava-bean roots have been turned under by hand to act as compost and nitrogen-fixing agents. He then plants, in the same rows, bush beans very close together. When these are picked, some bush-bean seeds are saved, usually in August; he then turns the bean plants under by hand to compost for the coming November fava-bean planting, in which he uses the composted fava beanstalks. He has also planted tomato seeds he has saved from the previous crop the year before. This has gone on for 60 years, and he has never had to buy a seed or seedling. Simply amazing. He is in his 90s now and in very good health. When I tell him how much I admire him, his comment is usually like, "Young man, which at 83 I love to hear, I'm only 93 now and planning on living to be 100 and plenty."

Another thing that had a profound impact on my gardening practices was when I read the book by John Jeavons and Carol Cox titled *The Sustainable Vegetable Garden*. They were the founders of the Ecology Action food-growing program. Their first book was titled *How to Grow More Vegetables* and is about their biointensive methods. There are many things I like about this book, including the beautiful cover and the handy size, so it can be used in the garden as a manual for easy reference. The actual contents cover what to grow and how to do it the biointensive way, composting, how to keep a garden healthy, and good detail on saving seeds. It has sold hundreds of thousands of copies and has seven translations. I highly recommend this book to all gardeners, no matter their level of experience.

CHAPTER 2

Seeds and Seedlings

There's an old saying that goes "When all else fails, read the directions." Of course, this was written by a company who markets vegetable seeds (just kidding). A great deal of what you need to know about planting seeds is on the back of every packet. There is a considerable number of pros and cons about whether to plant seeds or buy seedlings, which are small plants that are already growing. In the old days, buying seeds would give you a larger variety to choose from. Nowadays, I can go to most nurseries and find many varieties of seedlings available.

Tomatoes are a prime example. My two favorites are Better Boy and Celebrity. Both are hybrids, which are cross pollinated with another tomato variety, take a little more work, and are, therefore, more expensive, but available in most nurseries. Buying certain seeds may give you more variety in some categories, but trying to get a jump start may not be worth the cost in your water bill or the wait time to get the plant in the ground. If you plant seedlings directly into the soil, you can be assured of your spacing, whereas, if you planted seeds directly into the soil, some may not germinate; you would have to replant in those spaces.

Here is the information that is on the seed packet itself.

Description: The front of the packet will have the name of the company, the name of the variety, information on whether it's grown locally, USDA organically, and whether it's Heirloom. Information on the back of the packet: Planting season, ideal soil temperature, planting depth, how to sow, days to germinate, days to maturity, planting and watering methods, exposure (amount of sunlight), and how tall it grows.

Colorful and informative seed packets from San Diego Seed Company

Heirlooms, Hybrids, and GMOs

Heirloom seeds are open-pollinated seeds, which means they are naturally pollinated by hand, bird, wind, or insects; they are non-hybrid and usually passed down generationally. Seeds from these plants will produce the same characteristics as those of the parent plant.

Hybrid seeds result from crossing two parents of the same species in order to create a single generation. For example, my favorite tomatoes Better Boy and Celebrity are both award-winning hybrids bred for taste, appearance pest resistance. However, if you take their seeds and plant them, you probably won't get the same characteristics as the parent.

GMO (genetically modified organisms) are seeds in which the genetic material (DNA) has been altered in a way that does not occur naturally. It is done in a laboratory and is beyond the scope of my knowledge and this book. There is a lot of controversy on this subject and a plethora of information on this topic. I have read that 88% of the corn we eat is GMO, and, since corn is pollinated by wind, I don't know how tested it is for long-range safety purposes or if it will crossbreed with other species. With the ever-increasing population of our planet, this is definitely an important issue—one which many scientists believe could be the answer to the world hunger problem. The issue of whether GMOs are safe for the consumer is a topic of much debate and will likely go on for a long time.

CHAPTER 3

Soil, Air, Water, and Sun

Along with family and friends, gardening brings much joy and meaning to our everyday lives as well as some much-needed exercise. There is an old saying: "A little sweat never hurt anybody." It is also good for the immune system. If you look up the topics of perspiration and how it is linked with our immune systems, it's very interesting. There is also some research that shows contact with soil gives a positive immune response. Good soil structure is a function of how air, water, and sun all work together in a hopefully harmonious manner. It is important to try to mimic Mother Nature as closely as possible in our gardens. For instance, the top layer would be undecomposed organic matter (such as shredded leaves, grass clippings, and partially broken-down compost) on top of decomposed organic matter such as compost (lots of friability and air spaces) lying over topsoil that has not been tilled. Below all this would be a subsoil with no compaction. This will allow water and air to move up and down as needed. The goal is to have water and air available at all times for the soil organisms to stay healthy. If the soil is allowed to dry out from sun or wind, it causes things such as poor plant growth or leaf wilt. The soil organisms, which are important for producing life-giving chemicals to the roots, die off and are very difficult to bring back to their original state. Wind can be blocked by many means, such as walls, trees, and other types of vegetation. Too much sun can be bad for our crops, but, at the same time, a proper amount of sun is necessary. Plant leaves inhale air and the carbon from carbon dioxide, which is made into the sugars that is the final product of photosynthesis. Similarly, too much wind is not good, but no wind is bad, too, because it can cause plant leaves to be too large, which can take away from the fruit and vegetable growth.

Sunlight plays a crucial role, too. If you have too much leaf growth, not enough sunlight can reach the microclimate and smaller plants underneath. This reduces photosynthesis and the health of the plants. As mentioned, tillage is not good, because it disrupts the beneficial organisms. It is also important not to have long periods in which the soil lies unplanted (fallow), because of loss of fertility. Many plants such as radishes can be used to cover soils rapidly. When these faster-growing plants are harvested, the longer-growing and larger plants such as cucumbers, squash, and tomatoes will have more room to spread. Warmer soils are better for microbial growth, which means more nutrients will be available for your plants. Untilled soil that is aggregated and has lots of soil life heats up more easily.

CHAPTER 4

Power Planter

Hole Digging 101

The Power Planter is a back-saving, Swiss Army knife-type tool that can be used in many different applications around the home and garden. This steel auger fits into a 3/8-inch or ½-inch cordless hand drill and can be used to dig holes in even the hardest soil. When most people dig a hole, they reach for a spade, but for us "older" gardeners, the back-breaking work of digging holes to remove old plants or trees and plant new ones gets harder with each passing day. Augers have several advantages over other tools, including:

- they are easy to use, even for people with limited physical abilities

- they loosen the soil, making it easier for the roots to spread

- they require little physical effort to operate

The website for the Power Planter, www.PowerPlanter.com, contains a complete description of the auger, which is available in several different sizes, and detailed instructions for its many uses. From planting seeds and bulbs to removing old plants or trees with stubborn roots, this tool has revolutionized my gardening capabilities. It is also helpful for digging holes for fence posts and other home-and-garden improvements.

Turning the compost to aerate it is one of the more challenging things to do. Assembling the original compost pile, which is fairly lightweight work, is pretty easy, but turning the decomposing compost material can be heavy lifting, as you will see in the chapter on composting. The turning procedure using the model 324 (three inches wide by twenty-four inches long) is done by running it at very low speed,

Daughter Jeri using the Power Planter to turn compost

clockwise, using an in-and-out push-pull motion. Reaching all the way to the bottom of the pile, it basically turns the pile inside out, which is the goal.

Tilling can be another formidable task, especially in yards with compacted clay soil, like mine. The auger can be very useful in loosening compacted soil. The average depth of a one-level, brick (concrete-block) raised garden is eight inches, and a wood raised bed is ten inches. This is deep enough for many plants, but vine crops like pumpkins, winter squash, and watermelons are deep rooted, with roots that extend twenty-four to thirty-six or more inches. Artichokes, sweet potatoes, okra, and tomatoes are also deep rooted. Before the raised bed of any height is filled with soil, it can be tilled to a depth of several inches, which allows for the roots to grow much deeper, giving the gardener a wider range of plants that can be grown successfully in a raised bed.

The Power Planter auger has many more useful applications, which can be found on their website. If you decide to buy a Power Planter, be sure to watch the instructional video on their website. It's an easy-to-use device, but their directions for proper usage are most helpful.

CHAPTER 5

Compost Happens

Compost, in a nutshell, is organic matter that has been broken down. This natural process involves recycling organic matter, such as leaves, grass clippings, and food scraps and turning them into a valuable fertilizer that is rich in nutrients. Our friend from Australia says they have one of the original composters in his country. It is called a bush turkey, and, if you do an Internet search, you will see a big, beautiful bird that chases snakes and all sorts of creatures who are trying to invade its nests to steal eggs. They are so plentiful, running around the streets and supermarket parking lots, they are almost pests. The male builds a large pile of leaves by kicking its feet backwards. If the female likes his pile, she will accept him, otherwise, she runs off to find another guy who is a better builder. She lays her eggs in a hole at the top of the pile, and he tends things by increasing or decreasing the heat level by adding or removing leaves. When ready, the babies fly away, with no practice. Simply amazing!

Now back to the lower form of composting by humans. It is hard to believe that, in the 1940s, we had garbage collectors, who on a weekly basis picked up our garbage just like our present-day trash collectors. What a huge waste of this valuable "garbage." A large percentage of what goes into our garbage cans, namely, kitchen scraps and plant material, could be recycled through composting.

My homemade hot concrete-block composter

These days, we save all our kitchen scraps, except meat and bones, and if I don't have time to add it to my compost pile, it takes me only about one minute to dig a hole about eighteen inches deep with a Power Planter and bury the scraps. This is a fast-and-easy form of trench composting and can be done around my vegetables, trees, and flower beds.

Topsoil is a very important component of a healthy garden. It takes about 1000 years to form one inch of topsoil by erosion of rocks. Compost comes from decomposed organic material, is darker in color, and has lots of beneficial bacteria and fungi. Several methods are available to the gardener as to which ratio of ingredients to use. For many years, I just buried kitchen scraps and seaweed in long trenches. After about two

Raised-bed concrete-block cold composter

months, it was decomposed underground, and I could plant on top of that. When I began doing more container gardening and building raised beds, which required larger volumes of soil, I started using 100% store-bought potting soil, sometimes a combination of several brands mixed together. While these contain all kinds of premium ingredients, such as bat guano, dolomite, feather meal, sphagnum peat moss, forest products, and many other fine things, this can be quite expensive, especially when using containers, as one usually has to renew the soil each year. When I started above-ground composting, I built a concrete-block composter that had two four-foot-wide sections (three sixteen-inch bricks) four feet deep and forty inches high (five times the eight-inch height of each brick). The bricks were turned sideways to let air in. The four-by-eight-foot roof can be made of metal, fiberglass, or wood. Since we aren't bothered by critters, the front is made of fabric awning material (which can be bought at your local hardware store), attached to the top and to a two-by-four at the bottom. The top is hinged, but, usually, to gain access, I just flop the two-by-four up over the roof. Ideally, you want to locate your compost pile where the sun can reach it much of the day, as the heat from the sun will help accelerate the breakdown of the compost. Online, you will find many different kinds of composters, and this is one area in which you'll have to decide which is best suited for you.

What I do now seems to make my plants very happy. I make compost by collecting my grass lawn clippings, big bags of leaves from my neighbor's huge oak and ornamental pear trees, seaweed from our San Diego beaches (if no seaweed is available, I would buy seaweed meal at our nursery), and all manner of plant trimmings and kitchen scraps. It's good to run a lawn mower or leaf shredder over the leaves to increase the surface area so that the bacteria and fungi break it down faster. Ideally, it is recommended to have a 25:1 ratio of carbon to nitrogen, but I don't get too scientific about that. Be sure to layer the kitchen scraps with leaves and grass clippings. This ensures drainage and aeration of the decomposing material. I build this pile in layers with a pitchfork or shovel about six inches deep each and moisten each layer with water, to where it's like a wrung-out sponge. When I get a few layers built up, I then add the kitchen scraps, so they start out in the middle of the pile, just to keep it away from interested critters. The goal is to end up with a pile about four feet by four feet and four feet high. If it is only two or three feet high, not enough heat will build up to break things down. I then can start turning the pile in anywhere from three to thirty days with my Power Planter. You can actually turn it every two or three days to speed the process up and have compost in as little as one month. It will be a soft, crumbly mass and ready to use. Trying to turn it with a pitchfork is tough on the back, but using a Power Planter makes it so easy. When I use it, I employ the Power Planter in a slow in-and-out motion all the way to the bottom of the pile, which gently turns it inside out, and that is the goal. I try not to use a fast, jabbing motion, because it is too disruptive to the bacteria, fungi, and worms. After or during each turning session, I remoisten with water, because the organisms need water along with the induced air. Sometimes, if I have some old, previously used compost or soil, I will add a thin layer of this on the top of the pile. If the pile starts to have an unpleasant odor, you have probably added too much water, and the breakdown has gone from aerobic toward anaerobic. In this case, let the pile dry out for a while, or add a few more dry materials. Online, you will see a huge variety of techniques, but my very unscientific way works just fine.

CHAPTER 6

Raised Beds and Crop Rotation

Raised beds have many benefits for the backyard gardener. The greatest advantage is that it allows you to control what type of soil is used and gives you the flexibility to add amendments to only the ground where the planting and growing will take place. By having a narrow-enough bed that you can reach the middle from either side, the soil can be friable and non-compacted. By not having to walk on the soil, you are increasing the air spaces, which has many advantages, including oxygenation, moisture penetration, and drainage. A raised garden saves time and your back because it brings the garden more up to your level rather than you having to stoop down to its level. The ideal size is three to four feet wide, so that it is easy to reach across. Keeping it to about ten feet in length allows it to be more modular and manageable, to where it fits better in most garden spaces. Ideal depth depends on what type of plant you are growing. If you are growing crops like lettuce, a six-to-twelve-inch depth works out fine, but with crops like tomatoes, carrots, and other root crops whose roots reach deeper, two feet is better.

Concrete-block raised bed

The only tilling I ever do with a raised-bed garden is, before I add any soil, I till the native, existing soil with a Power Planter, which gives me an extra six to twelve inches of depth. I try to plant like vegetables next to similar varieties; this allows me to keep track of things easier and be better organized for deep, shallow, or irregular watering.

I've done some not-so-smart planting in the past, for instance, planting a low crop such as lettuce or swiss chard next to a very high crop such as corn, which shades out the lower crops. Another mistake I have made is planting pole beans or even cucumbers, which will sometimes wrap around items such as corn that was planted too close to them.

Crop rotation is an area where you may want to do some experimenting, and I am still in the process of learning what is best. For instance, some schools of thought feel that, when you remove a particular plant, you can just replace it with some new soil and a new plant. The other is that you should not plant, for example, tomatoes, in the same bed they were in previously because the soil may be contaminated with soil-borne bacteria or fungi that led to a poor harvest. The chances of this happening are much less when planting in a different bed, even though it may not be new soil. Life will be easier if you can do this successfully and replace most or all of your soil at one time.

As far as building materials for raised beds goes, after using raised beds for more than sixty years, I like to use concrete blocks that are sixteen inches long by eight inches wide by eight inches high, with two five-inch-by-five-inch spaces in each one. For shallow plants, one layer is high enough, but for deeper-rooted plants, I like to use two layers, making it sixteen inches high, plus I can plant in the five-inch spaces separately. I have used two-inch-by-ten-inch redwood in the past, and these have lasted forty-five years but cost about four times more than concrete blocks and are not as easy to kneel or sit on. A four-foot-by-four-foot, single-layer concrete-block raised bed would cost about $18, but redwood would cost around $80, although it would be two inches higher. Cedar would last several years in most climates and be cheaper. Less-expensive wood would probably last about four years. Another thing I like about concrete, in addition to its being the most durable, is that it acts as a wonderful insulator and warms your seeds and plants more easily, giving you a jump-start on planting. I only recently discovered Behlen Country one piece all metal raised beds in many shapes and sizes. They are containers with bottoms in which you will have to drill drainage holes. I purchased four from Home Depot and I am hoping these will be the best addition to my garden in many years.

CHAPTER 7

Container Gardening

There are many different types of containers, which are basically a small, raised bed. They often need more watering, but this can be modified by various means. There are many advantages to container gardening. One of the main ones is that pests such as earwigs, slugs, and snails have a difficult time accessing the plants and their fruits and vegetables. Containers are especially useful for growing berries such as strawberries if you do not wish to share your fruit with slugs and snails. Growing in containers also allows you to completely control the growing medium, adding amendments and nutrients that would be beneficial to that specific plant.

Self-watering pots have a compartment in the bottom which holds water and allows moisture to be drawn up through the roots. These pots are usually plastic and, being poorly insulated, would ordinarily need more-than-usual watering. These may be helpful to people who do not have the time to constantly monitor the moisture in their soil.

Fabric containers have been around only a few years and have become very popular because of their light weight and portability. They come in many different sizes, and most have handles. Some of the

Grow Bags filled with lettuce and broccoli in Jeri's garden

advantages are that the roots are self-pruning, they release heat easily, they prevent circling roots, and the material porosity and breathability aerate the root zone.

Oak barrels with fava beans

Ceramic pots are best for plants like plumerias and other succulents, because they drain easily and do not hold water.

While there are many beautiful terra-cotta (clay) pots, most of them are unglazed on the inside and will absorb the water out of the soil like a dry sponge. They should be used only for plants that do well in dry, well-drained soil such as cactus and succulents.

Wood containers range from hanging baskets to old whiskey barrels to raised beds. Many people find they can repurpose wood from doors and houses to create wood structures, and old wine barrels have been used for years for container gardening. In this day of recycling and repurposing, almost anything that is safe to grow food in can be used to grow fruits and vegetables, as long as one can drill drainage holes in the bottom and it is deep enough for the roots. I have even seen people growing plants in an old pair of cowboy boots . . . now that is repurposing!

CHAPTER 8

Irrigation

I hope you don't find this subject too dry. Growing up, I spent many hours watering the family organic garden with a hose, by hand. Everything was in raised beds and double dug, followed by long rows (canals), down which the water would flow. It was a very effective system, but by today's standards, it did waste water and time. For many years after that I used every type of irrigation system imaginable—large sprinklers, 1/4-inch tubing with mini-sprinklers, bubblers, and various drip systems. My newest system that I'm presently installing has me really excited because of its efficiency, labor, and water savings. I first heard about it in a book by Robert Kourik titled *Lazy-Ass Gardening* and also on a YouTube channel called "Next Level Gardening." Both have a huge range of gardening information. If you have ever had your own drip system, you have probably discovered that they are very efficient but have quite a few parts that can clog and break and need constant repairing. This new drip irrigation system consists of a new type of 1/4-inch inline emitter tubing made by a company called Netafim. The tubing is Techline (R)HCVXR Landscape Dripline, with copper oxide built into every emitter. The copper prevents root intrusion. Emitters come in various flow rates (I'm starting with the 1/2 gallon per hour) and at different distances apart (in my case, twelve inches). The Netafim website lists all the needed tubing and parts. The way the setup works is that a controller screws onto your water or hose attachment, followed by a pressure regulator, which, in turn, is followed by 1/2-inch tubing that goes (in a trench underground if you wish) to your garden, in my case to my raised beds. A hole is punched in the 1/2-inch tubing to receive the 1/4-inch tubing, which is placed wherever you wish it to be. Some of my raised gardens are three feet wide and up to twenty feet long. The setup will be to run the 1/2-inch tubing up and across the three-foot width and branch twenty-foot-long emitters tubing for each row of plants (e.g, corn). The 1/2-inch tubing will bend around corners only a small amount without kinking, so elbows may be needed. The various fittings are all pressure fittings, so you just have to push the hose into them. The new controllers are very high-tech and come with features such as moisture meters and weather-system sensors.

How Often and Deep to Water

According to Robert Kourik, who has written a book on the subject, daily irrigation with very tiny amounts of water is the best and promotes the greatest growth and yield. The idea is to keep the soil slightly damp. Yet, this may not be true for all plants, and here is where it is important to remember the cardinal rule of gardening: KNOW YOUR PLANTS. When it comes to how much water, how often, what amendments they may need, and where to plant them, some plants need six to eight hours of full sun to thrive and develop fruit, while others can do with some shade and placement in cooler areas of the garden. Each plant variety is different, and you will increase your gardening success by knowing these things in advance. If you start your plants from seed, almost everything you need to know to get the plant started is on that tiny little packet—how deep to plant the seed for best germination, how moist to keep the soil, how far apart to thin the plants once they sprout, etc. If you buy starter plants from the nursery, some information is on that tiny plastic marker usually inserted into the soil of each container. The rest can be found in the many gardening-resource books available, such as the *Sunset Western Garden Book of Gardening* and Pat Welsh's *Southern California Organic Gardening*, two of my favorites. The YouTube channel has hundreds of videos made by gardening experts all over the world that cover a large variety of topics, including specific plants, irrigation, composting, etc. By knowing your plants, you can plan ahead and plant the plants together that have the same water requirements. Tomatoes need plenty of good air flow around them for optimum health, so, when planting them, consider whether they are determinate or indeterminate in placing them into the ground. I have too often placed them too close together when they were tiny starter plants only to find the indeterminate ones can become a jungle if not staked up as they grow. Once they are planted and spaced properly, you can water them using the same technique for all of them.

CHAPTER 9

The Dirt on Potting Soil

Potting soil is a critical factor in determining the health and ultimate yield and success of your plants. Sure, you can grab a bag of cheap potting soil, and chances are your marigolds will do fine. However, for gardens which produce fruit and vegetables, the results will vary widely, depending upon the soil you plant them in.

I grow a lot of corn, tomatoes, and succulents, including plumerias, in all of which proper irrigation and soil type play a large role. For instance, corn and tomatoes need a lot of water, although not necessarily the same way. Plumerias are more finicky and easily overwatered, which will cause rot and, ultimately, death. All this means that one type of potting soil does not fit all and is where the individual components are important. As you would read a label on a food product you are buying, reading the label on the potting soil is just as important. This also means you need to know your plants' soil and irrigation requirements before putting them into the ground. Succulents, including plumerias, should be planted in a cactus-mix potting soil that has good drainage. Components in potting soil that allow for good drainage are perlite, sand, pumice, and pea gravel, to name a few. Perlite and pumice act as an aggregate spacer to allow drainage, which these plants require. However, pumice is a natural product that is heavier than perlite, which tends to float to the surface and allows compaction. The following is a list of ingredients of common potting soil that vary quite a bit from brand to brand.

Common Ingredients and What They Contribute

Some of the potting soils are proprietary, which means, even though the ingredients are listed, the amounts and formulations are not. Through trial and error, you can decide which ones work best for you. It is always a good idea when handling growing mediums to use gloves and a mask. Most potting soils are referred to as soilless mediums, because they contain no soil. In the following ingredient list, not all of these are found in potting soils at one time.

1. Pumice—Discussed above. It's heavier than perlite, so it stays mixed in your soil and won't float to the top. It resists decomposition, so it hardly ever needs replacing, unlike coir and peat moss.

2. Perlite—Discussed above.

3. Coir—A byproduct of coconut husks, ecofriendly, with good water retention. It is fibrous and does not compact easily, leaving space for healthy roots and good aerobic airspaces for nutrient and water uptake; has reusability aspects, sometimes used in conjunction with peat moss and perlite. Coir is organic and, unlike peat moss, a completely renewable resource.

4. Vermiculite—A material created when mica is mined and heated until it forms small particles that contain air spaces, which can

hold a lot of water. When used with potting soils, the mixture becomes friable and loose, which creates an atmosphere that is good for plant root growth.

It is dry and dusty, like many of these ingredients, so, again, be sure to wear a particle mask, gloves, and long-sleeved shirt.

5. Peat Moss—Comes from prehistoric bogs and is a nonrenewable resource. It makes your mixtures lighter and improves friability and its ability to retain water.

6. Worm castings—See vermiculture chapter.

7. Feather meal—Made from grinding poultry feathers using heat and pressure, and then drying. Temperatures are high enough to cook and sterilize the feathers, which are ground into a powder for use as a nitrogen source.

8. Bat Guano—Used in many soil amendments due to its high content of nitrogen, phosphorus, and potassium. If you are worried about health issues with this or any of these products, be sure to do your own research. I have been assured by one of the larger compost companies that they sterilize any questionable ingredients.

9. Seabird Guano—Not as potent as bat guano but high in phosphorus.

10. Crab meal—Made from grinding up crab skeletons; very high in phosphorus, nitrogen, and magnesium.

11. Kelp meal—Ground up and dehydrated seaweed; contains many nutrients for healthier plants.

12. Alfalfa meal—Made from dehydrated and ground alfalfa; takes nitrogen from the air and holds it in its roots.

13. Oyster shell lime—Ground-up oyster shells; raises the pH in acidic soils.

14. Dolomite lime—From deposits of calcium carbonate. Added magnesium makes it a very effective pH raiser.

15. Fishbone meal—Made from ground-up fishbones; full of phosphorus, calcium, nitrogen, and many trace elements.

16. Wetting agent—Usually made from parts of the yucca plant; allows plants to better utilize water and nutrients.

17. Gypsum—Helps to break down clay soils; be sure to study the use of gypsum online, because it may have quite a few negative impacts.

18. Some potting-soil companies have various amounts and types of bacteria and fungi in their potting soil.

19. Aged forest products—Add to composting.

Essential Elements

Plants require sixteen elements for normal growth and in different amounts. Too little of these elements can negatively impact their development and flowering/fruit-bearing capacity, and too much can be toxic to the plants. Toxic levels of nonessential elements such as aluminum and arsenic are harmful. The first result of nutritional deficiency, toxicity, or imbalance is a reduction in plant growth, either visible or invisible (under the radar, so to speak), but yields are restricted nevertheless.

Soil and Plant-Tissue Tests

Most home gardeners are familiar with soil tests, such as pH for acidic and alkaline levels. Commercial farmers are very interested in tests that give them better-quality crops and yields. This means they need test not only the soil but also the plant tissue itself, such as corn leaves. More and more people are becoming interested in how all this plays out with their own home gardening and immunity issues. For instance, aluminum is the most common element on Earth and is ubiquitous in the soil. Research shows that aluminum levels in the body affect certain health problems such as Alzheimer's and Parkinson's Disease. Much of this information can be found online at various universities' extensions. One of the best comes from Purdue University. This information, through plant analysis, helps farmers with decisions on fertilizer effectiveness and the need for additional nutrients.

Plant Analysis

This is the quantitative determination of the elements in plant tissue. Plant analysis usually analyzes nitrogen (N), phosphorus (P), potassium (K), calcium (Ca), magnesium (Mg), sulfur (S), iron (Fe), manganese (Mn), copper (Cu), zinc (Zn), and boron (B). Aluminum and sodium are sometimes included, even though they are not essential elements. Aluminum can be toxic in acid soils, and sodium improves the quality of some crops such as beets and celery. Plant analysis is distinguished from tissue testing, in that it is a quantitative laboratory analysis, whereas tissue testing is a quick type of test of plant sap, carried out in the field. Plant analysis is unique from other crop diagnostic tests, in that it gives an overall picture of the nutrient levels within the plant at the time the sample was taken.

Summary

Plant analysis is a wonderful tool for confirming nutrient deficiencies, toxicities, and imbalances. If you wish to do a simple soil test or go further with plant analysis, there are many companies that do this and can be found online.

CHAPTER 10

Wonderful Worms

When our daughter mentioned this book should have a vermiculture chapter, it didn't take long to "wriggle" into the subject, even though my knowledge of worms was very limited. Jeri, who has had her own organic fruit and vegetable garden for more than twenty years, has also had her own worm bin for as many years. This inspired me to learn about these slimy, wriggly little creatures. I bought a book called *Worms Eat My Garbage*, followed by *The Worm Book*, co-authored by the late Loren Nancarrow, who had a wonderful San Diego TV gardening show for many years. Worms are fascinating creatures and so important to the composting web. I must apologize to my newfound worm friends for such inconsiderate childish songs such as "Worms crawl in and worms crawl out, and worms play pinochle on your snout" and "Nobody likes me anymore, so I think I will eat some worms." Here are some of the interesting things I have learned.

Why Are Worms Important?

There are more than 6,000 species of worms, and they are found all over the world. They eat, sleep, mate (each worm has both male and female reproductive organs), and poop all in the same place and, by doing so, can greatly improve the quality of the soil. The amount of fertilizer they add is less than that from compost, but the quality of the soil is greatly improved by their presence. Their poop or worm castings add micronutrients such as calcium, magnesium, and sulphur, and are full of plant-growth promoters. Worm castings have a higher percentage of humus than compost or soil, and studies have shown they improve the soil structure so much that seed germination is improved, and yields can be greatly enhanced. The worm's aeration of the soil also helps improve water penetration, and nutrients are better assimilated by the plant roots.

The Soil

Soils can be soft, sandy, or sticky and clay-like. In any case, it takes about a thousand years of rock erosion to make an inch of soil. Soil also contains decaying plant and animal (organic) matter called humus, which is a byproduct of the worms' breaking everything down, making for healthy soil. The castings contain bacteria and animal and plant matter, which continue to be composted and supply important nutrients for the plants.

Worm Anatomy and Biology

Charles Darwin studied earthworms for a great part of his life. He found them absolutely critical and very important to the history of the world. Worms may have come about during the Jurassic period and have likely been on Earth 120 million years. Earthworm bodies are composed of segments. They have no teeth or eyes but can sense light and dark. Very small particles of food enter the mouth, go through the pharynx, esophagus, and crop, are ground up by the gizzard, and continue through the intestine and out the anus in the form of castings.

Worm Bins and Maintenance

Most vermiculture involves various types of worms, usually red wigglers in an enclosed bin, where the worms break down kitchen scraps and other materials. These bins come in many different sizes and shapes; more information on these structures can be found online. San Diego weather lends itself to outdoor vermicomposting, which also allows one to have a large bin and compost more worm castings. Except for my fruit trees and a few inground tomatoes, I utilize four raised beds for our vegetables and one for vermicomposting only. By using raised beds, I can fill them with lots of different composting materials such as those listed under "Compost Happens" earlier in this book. This is termed

Jeri's repurposed cooler worm bin

"cold composting" because no heat builds up to harm the worms, the good and bad bacteria, and fungi. Did you know what one mushroom said to the other? "When you get to know me, I'm a funguy."

Worms wiggling inside

Back to the very serious and exciting subject of worms. The reason no heat builds up is because the compost piles are only about two feet high and spread over a large surface area, which is normally about four feet wide and eight feet long. This allows the worms to do all the work; no human-powered tilling or turning is necessary. I fill the raised beds with composting materials and worms, and, as castings are produced along with compost and probably some un-broken-down composting materials, I plan to plant my vegetables. This way, the composting process can continue as the plants grow. The worms have a constant supply of food, as I bury my kitchen scraps weekly, including vegetable peelings, overripe fruit, bread crusts, etc. I bury the new composting materials in a side trench, away from the plants and any new crops to be planted. If it is time not to plant for a while, I will add new worm-food materials and let the worms roam freely.

Bedding

Bedding materials for my outdoor bin consist mostly of composted plant materials, but you can add a bottom layer of leaves, grass clippings, newspaper, or straw before adding the dirt or potting soil and compost.

Bin Types

Our daughter is all about recycling and sustainability. She used an old cooler with a lid and wheels, drilled holes in the sides at the top for air, and has harvested many generations of worms and many pounds of worm castings. She gave me a bucket full of worms from her bin to get mine started. Although many varieties of worm gardens are sold commercially, it is easy to make your own in a raised bed or use an older, recycled container, as she did. They just need a place to stay cool and moist, and breathe; worms can easily be fed kitchen scraps. She was given a can full of worms by her neighbor and has never had to add since. Every so often, she scoops up some of the castings along with a few worms and scatters them in her own garden, which is mostly fruit trees, tomatoes, blueberries, and a few containers for seasonal vegetables.

In indoor and outdoor bins, most people feed the worms with kitchen scraps. These can be supplemented with coffee grounds, rice, stale-bread products, melon rinds, and crushed eggshells. Stay away from citrus, meats and bones, dairy products, salts and fats, pet poop, and fireplace ashes. The worm gizzards need grit to help grind up the food. The grit consists of small particles of soil. In container-types of bins, add a little bit of soil for this purpose (our daughter saves all her old potting soil to add to her worm bin as needed).

Pathogens

If you're worried about E. coli, salmonella, or other pathogens in your worm bin, here is some of the latest scientific information on the subject. It is believed that bad bacteria can be neutralized or eaten by the more numerous good bacteria, so there is hardly ever a problem, even though we don't know the exact reasons for this. Research is showing that the worm's digestive system is able to destroy these pathogens to levels below health-department guidelines. However, this research is not conclusive, and the Environmental Protection Agency recommends composting anything you might feel is contaminated at high temperatures—160 degrees Fahrenheit for three days. This would kill any worms in the process, so this should be done before adding worms.

Always practice good hygiene by wearing gloves and washing your hands and tools when working with worm composting systems.

CHAPTER 11

If a Tomato Could Talk

If a tomato could talk (in tomatoese, of course), the conversation might go like this. "I'm really ticked off because these darn humans are once again messing with my genetics. They actually cut me in half and made a potato out of my lower half. They call it 'grafting.' I call it 'major surgery.' Just because we are both in the nightshade family, they have no right to do this without my permission. I feel so psychologically damaged, I'm thinking of speaking to my attorney. Mostly because they had the gall to call me a POMATO and put me up for sale in stores—how embarrassing! Another thing that really gets my goat is that, once again, my genetics are on the line. Most people don't know whether I'm a fruit or a vegetable, even though the U.S. Supreme Court, in 1895, declared me a vegetable. So, even though I am botanically a fruit, politically, I'm a vegetable. However, I've been around for a million years, and I'm still KING OF THE GARDEN."

Tomatoes are warm-season plants. In San Diego, we do not have much concern with frost, but I usually wait for late spring to plant them.

In your area, you should wait about one week after the last frost to plant for best success. Planting in raised beds allows for good drainage using good compost. For the last several years, I have planted my two favorite

Better Boy tomato out of hand

varieties, which are "Better Boy," an indeterminate, which means they grow very tall but can be pruned low enough to be able to pick the fruit, and they keep producing after picking. The second one is called "Celebrity" and is a determinate, which means it's lower and bushier, and doesn't keep producing. Both are big award winners and disease resistant. I try to plant at least one other variety. This year it was "Sun Sugar." My friend Joe Barry started these from seed on July 1, and, as of December 1, they are still producing. They have thin skins, as opposed to most cherry types and are now my favorite-tasting tomato. I plant again

the author with his tomato bounty

around the 1st of July and again August 1st. A new superstar on the block is "Bodacious," so it will be included next year. The old saying about a tomato a day keeps the doctor away certainly is true here. They are great immune boosters and loaded with vitamins C and A, plus lycopene—all great antioxidants. It is good to keep the soil moist, but don't overwater, to avoid fungal diseases. Morning watering is best, so plants dry out, but if time does not allow that, always keep water low and off plants. With their deep roots, it is best to water longer and let it soak into the soil so it reaches the root and does not water only the topsoil. Plant in full sun, as this increases their chances of resisting diseases. They do well in a mixture of 50/50 composted and good topsoil or 1/3 each of compost, vermiculite, and peat moss. I have had good luck with straight, high-quality potting soils like E. B. Stone's 420. They are heavy feeders, and the important ingredients tend to get used up every three weeks or so, so I spread more of these planting materials all around. Lack of calcium can cause Blossom-End Rot, which many people who grow tomatoes have experienced. A dose of Epsom salts, which are high in magnesium, helps to make the calcium in the soil available for absorption. I also grind up all my leftover eggshells and add those to the soil.

Tomato hornworm

Tomato hornworms, the caterpillars of the five-spotted hawkmoth, can chew up a plant very fast. Look for stems that have been decimated, with the leaves missing. Another telltale sign is their black droppings. As a preventative, you can spray with the organic bacteria BT (Bacillus thuingiensis) spray. If you find them already enjoying the fruits of your labors and are not willing to share (they can consume an entire plant in a short time) you can remove them by hand (yuck). I would like to have a nickel for every time I have heard someone say, "Nothing tastes better than a fresh vine-ripened tomato." Make that a quarter.

CHAPTER 12

Corn

Corn was the main crop grown and consumed during the civilization of the Americas. We have fossil evidence that it was grown
in North America 4,000 years ago. Yellow corn is higher in carotene
lutein than white corn, making the yellow variety better for eyesight. It
has many phytonutrients that are health promoting. Its thiamine gives
you more energy and is a neurotransmitter for better neuro-function. It
is rich in antioxidants, which help prevent many diseases.

Sweet corn is grown by most gardeners. It retains more sugar in the
kernels than other types of corn. Fresh, just-picked corn, in my opinion,
is as good as a fresh-picked tomato. It's easier to grow and, like tomatoes,
is a warm-weather vegetable (it's actually in the grass family). My favorite
way to eat it is raw or slightly cooked. It's fun to show children how
each of the many silk threads coming out the top go to each individual
kernel of corn.

In San Diego, with our fairly warm summer weather, it's not hard
to have two crops in succession starting in late spring. I've always grown

corn in raised gardens. For instance, if the raised garden is four feet by four feet, which gives me sixteen square feet, I am able to plant sixteen corn stalks. Each stalk will have at least one ear—and often two ears—so

Raised bed with cornstalks

we get roughly twenty-five ears per planting, which gives plenty of room for the roots. I've had good luck with 100% E. B. Stone 420 potting soil or other potting soils mixed with my homemade compost 50–50. Corn is pollinated by the wind, so it's best not to plant one long, single row but to have several plants or rows of plants next to each other. Corn prefers slightly acidic pH soil, with seven being neutral. So, if it's below 5.5, it's good to add some dolomite or lime to raise the pH. Plant the seeds about one inch deep. My recent experience has been the best with Top Hat corn from San Diego Seed Company. These seeds are quite large compared to other varieties, so if it came to the point where I could not get this size, I would buy several packets of different brands and try the large ones first.

Harvest of Top Hat corn from San Diego Seed

Watering

Corn needs plenty of water, especially when they are young and developing their root systems. The rule of thumb is about one to two inches per week, depending on weather. Water stress during pollination can result in deformed ears or missing kernels. Contrary to popular belief, sweet corn, once established, can use minimal water if well mulched, which greatly helps retain the moisture in the soil. A drip system works best, but a soaker hose also works.

Fertilizing

Corn plants need lots of nitrogen to grow and yield. In the seed stage of development, the corn plant has taken in 10% of the nitrogen it will need. By the time of flowering, it will have taken in 65%. A shortage of nitrogen can cause reduced ear-size formation and less potential yield. During the rapid-growth stage, the corn will absorb up to eight pounds of nitrogen per day per acre. Therefore, fertilizing with nitrogen-rich ingredients is critical when growing corn. Every three to six weeks, I add some fresh compost or potting soil to replenish what has been lost through watering and absorption. Generally speaking, the corn will be ready to harvest when the silk becomes brown and dry. To avoid breaking off a stalk, support the stalk with one hand, and bend the ear of corn downwards with the other hand.

Do's and Don'ts

Don't plant different types of corn together—it will reduce the corn quality.

Pests and Critters

Corn earworms lay their eggs on the silk, and the larvae burrow into the kernels. My way of taking care of this is to spray the silk thoroughly with water when I first see the small, black eggs appearing. Do this early in the morning so that the silk can dry out. I rarely have this problem and have never had to resort to any form of pesticide.

Our neighborhood has lots of raccoons, which love even young corn. However, I've never had a raccoon problem, and I attribute that to my wife's many solar lighting decorations all over the yard (raccoons are nocturnal). Crows are plentiful in our area, along with lots of smaller birds, all of which can decimate young corn plants very quickly. My solution to this has been successful: string a row of old CDs along the entire row, plus in one area of the yard. I also have a fake turkey, an owl, and a hawk, which may help.

CHAPTER 13

Beets

B eets are known for their immune-system boosting and anticancer effects. They contain large amounts of vitamin C and B9, and the mineral content of consists of potassium, phosphorous, manganese, and iron. In other words, not only are they sweet, delicious, and easy to grow in the garden, but they are good for you, too. Because they have fairly long roots, they do best in a raised bed in well-composted and good-draining soil. Beets are a perfect choice to grow in the cool weather of fall, winter, and spring. If planting seeds, use several seeds, and, when the seedlings are several inches tall, thin them out to about six inches apart. It is best to side-dress them every few weeks with compost mixed with worm castings, and a drink of water-soluble organic fertilizer is always helpful.

Organically grown beets from San Diego Seed Company

CHAPTER 14

Beans

I n our garden, we grow a lot of beans, including bush beans, pole, and yellow wax beans in the summer. In the fall, winter, and spring, we grow fava beans, which are high in protein and contain many vitamins, including vitamin A, and many minerals, including B6, phosphorous, iron, and calcium. Pole beans are climbers and need to be trellised. Be sure to keep away from other plants such as corn and tomatoes, as they will use them for a climbing structure and entangle everything in sight. Bush beans are great for the home gardener with limited space, as they can easily be grown in containers on decks or patios and do not require any support structures. Fava beans are huge in size and are popular in Mediterranean countries. They are my favorite, eaten raw or cooked, but can also be frozen or dried for storage. They do have some possible negative health issues, as people lacking in a specific enzyme can become ill. You should discuss with a health professional and study online for further information on this subject.

Huge fava beans

Beautiful fava bean flowers

Fava bean plants in raised beds

CHAPTER 15

Raphanus Raphanistrum Sativus . . .

Or . . . Radishes

Radishes are an easy-to-grow root vegetable in the Brassica cabbage family. They are fast and easily germinated and can be grown in just about any container. They are a favorite with the home gardener, who has so many choices of varieties and colors ranging from white and red to purple. They grow best in cooler weather and can be grown year-round, with care to keep away from too much heat in summer. It is easy to plant successive crops using a different variety each time. Radishes are rich in vitamin C and potassium and may play a positive role in the immune system. The low-calorie, crunchy little tuber makes it a perfect snack and a colorful addition to salads.

Colorful seed packet from San Diego Seed Company

Radish seeds germinating in a grow bag

CHAPTER 16

Squash

S quash is easy to grow and does best in warmer weather. It does not grow well in cooler weather, and many varieties are subject to powdery mildew. Full sun is the key here. The many varieties have large leaves and can take up a lot of space when grown in the ground. A great alternative is to grow them up a supporting structure such as a pole, teepee, or trellis—and keep the leaves pruned a bit. This keeps the fruit off the ground and allows more air flow, limiting the chances of powdery mildew and easier access to the fruit. Winter squash such as butternut, acorn, and Kabocha, to name a few, can be grown and easily stored for months due to their hard shell. The softer, more delicate squash, such as summer squash and zucchini, can be grown and eaten during the late spring and summer. The many varieties make it a versatile fruit that can be used in countless ways. It is high in vitamins C and B, as well as in many minerals, such as manganese, potassium, and others. Next

Thanksgiving, keep in mind that a single serving of pumpkin pie contains twenty percent of the RDA for vitamin B12 and niacin, fifteen percent of vitamin K, and lots of other vitamins and minerals. In other words, have another slice!

Multi-colored pattypan squash

Seeds from Renee's Garden are color-coded with USDA food-grade stain to distinguish varieties.

CHAPTER 17

Peaches and Stone Fruit

It is hard to beat the taste of a tree-ripened peach in the middle of summer, but apricots and plums are not far behind. Peaches, plums, apricots, nectarines, mangoes, and cherries are all called "stone fruits" because of the pit or "stone" contained in their center, which is actually their seed. While these fruits grow on trees, there are also other stone fruits such as watermelon, raspberries, blackberries, and mulberries that you may not typically think of as stone fruit. Even olives, almonds, and coconuts are considered stone fruit. Peaches and their soft-skinned friends are a great source of vitamins A and C, which are antioxidants that stabilize free radicals, which are associated with cancer and many medical problems. Many peach-tree varieties have a high-chill requirement and do not grow well in our subtropical climate in Southern California. There are, however, low-chill varieties that do very well here, including August Pride, Mid Pride, and Eva's Pride. Artic Star and Snow Queen, both of which our daughter has her in backyard, all produce deliciously sweet nectarines, with the white flesh ones from Artic Star being the sweetest.

Jeri's peach tree

CHAPTER 18

Guava

Guavas are a small tree in the Myrtle family with soft, delicious fruit, native to tropical and subtropical countries. We have three varieties that grow and produce fruit throughout the year in three different periods, so that we have ripe guavas all year round. Our three varieties are African, pineapple, and lemon guavas. Guavas are loaded with vitamin C (209 percent Daily Values, as compared to an orange, which is only 85 percent) and phytonutrients, all of which are good immune boosters. They also contain tons of potassium (about 230 mg per fruit) and many healthful minerals that may protect against different types of cancer. All three varieties will stand a light frost, and, as I am writing this, in March 2021, our African guava is loaded with dozens of tennis-ball size fruits. I purchased this tree from Walter Andersen Nursery when it was four feet tall, and, a year later, it was six feet tall and very productive. If any of my guava trees start to show any signs of pests, as with most of my other fruit trees, I just spray them with water in the morning, and that usually takes care of them.

African Guavas

CHAPTER 19

Cherimoya

Cherimoyas are a South American fruit normally pollinated by special indigenous insects. It grows well in the U.S. in warmer, more tropical areas, such as Southern California. Due to the limited growing area and delicate nature of the fruit, it tends to be very expensive to buy in markets. It presently costs about $7 a pound and can be found in some specialty-produce and farmers markets. It is referred to by many as "God's Fruit" and is my personal favorite. I usually let them sit on the kitchen counter until they are slightly soft and then peel it and spoon out the delicious custard-like interior, which tastes like a combination of mango, banana, and papaya. I usually prune the three trees in early spring, hand-pollinate around June, and harvest in December. Locally, they are lightly pollinated by the wind, but it's best done by hand. This involves using a camel-hair brush, taking pollen from the flower in the male stage, and dabbing it in the same flower or other flowers when they open up and are in the female stage. Their pollen can be stored in the refrigerator for a few nights.

El Bumpo Cherimoya

While researching the cherimoya chapter I found the following which I felt you should know but be sure to do your own research on the subject. Cherimoya belongs to the genus annonin. Some fruits in this genus have been known to cause neurological health problems such as Parkinson's Disease.

CHAPTER 20

Peppers

All types of peppers are part of the genus *Capsicum* and include hot varieties, known as chili peppers, and the sweet varieties, such as bell peppers. Peppers are a great source of vitamins A and C, which help fight free radicals. They are easy to grow, and I usually mix them in with eggplants and swiss chard because they take the same amount of water and are about the same size. Peppers grow well in raised beds, containers, and in the ground, and need to be planted in full sun. They are light feeders, and you can side-dress or drench with organic water-soluble fertilizer but not too much nitrogen, as they will grow leafy and not have much fruit production. Most sweet peppers mature in 60 to 90 days, but hot peppers can take up to 150 days. Peppers are versatile, in that they can be eaten raw or cooked in food and also frozen, dried, or pickled. How many pecks of pickled peppers did Peter Piper pick?

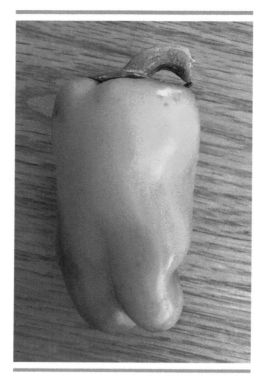

Peppers from our garden

Peppers from our garden

CHAPTER 21

Figs

Figs are the fruit of the ficus tree, which is part of the mulberry family. They are mentioned in the Bible and other ancient writings and are thought to have originally been cultivated in Egypt. They were then introduced to the Mediterranean by the ancient conquerors. In the late 19th century, when Spanish missionaries established the mission in San Diego, California, they planted fig trees.

Fig trees are very easy to grow and, once they get started, almost impossible to remove. We once had five fig trees because we wanted to try different varieties. The birds loved all the figs, but they just got out of hand, so we decided to keep the three that we like the best and remove the other two. The problem is you cannot just cut a fig tree off close to the ground, because within six months, it will grow back and start producing figs again. I have mentioned, in the grafting section, that we now have one fig tree on which were grafted three different varieties of figs.

Figs range in color, texture, and flavor, depending on the variety. Some of the more popular ones are Black Mission, Kadota, Calimyra,

Brown Turkey, and Adriatic. Figs are a very healthy addition to your diet and can be prepared in many different ways, including in salads, eaten alone, put in baked goods, or made into jams. They are full of potassium, which is linked to the lowering of blood pressure. They are known to have good dietary fiber, which helps in digestion and regulates cholesterol and blood-sugar levels.

Figs and other summer fruits from Jeri's garden

CHAPTER 22

Dragon Fruit

These plants are a large, tall, climbing succulent native to Central and South America that produce an exotic-looking yellow or pinkish-red fruit. Pitahaya or Pitaya, also known as Dragon Fruit, has become popular in recent years in juice bars and health-food restaurants and is often used to make fruit bowls and smoothies. The bright-pink variety is sold frozen in most grocery stores and makes a delicious and beautiful smoothie. The fruit can be either white or magenta inside and is full of immune boosters, vitamins, and minerals. The fruit starts out as a gigantic, fragrant white flower that opens for just one night. Bats and moths pollinate the flowers in their native lands. In San Diego, either bees or wind can pollinate it, or it can be done by hand-pollinating with a camel-hair brush to move the pollen from the male part to the female. Ripe fruits average about one pound and are a sight to behold. Like cherimoyas, they can be quite expensive.

Dragon Fruit's dramatic colorful outside

Inside of the Dragon Fruit

CHAPTER 23

Smitten by Succulents

When we decided to sell the house we built 45 years ago and downsize to a smaller, single-story home, we knew we would need to beautify the exterior in order to optimize our chances to sell it. Our view of the city of San Diego and the bay was beautiful, but the house was dated, and the front bank, which was planted many years ago with ivy and needed constant weeding and water, did nothing for its curb appeal. The city had imposed water restrictions due to very low rainfall, and we were considering planting a drought-resistant landscape.

Succulents were becoming popular in our county, and we decided to do some research to see if they would work for our landscape. Our first stop was to admire a house up the street that had gorgeous succulents and outstanding boulders and rocks. Our second stop was at Solana Succulents in north San Diego County. The owner, Jeff Moore, made some nice suggestions for a start on our project. We also bought the first two books he had written about succulents, along with some beautiful plants. I found out later that Jeff is well known for his use of succulents to make underwater garden scenes. He creates undersea landscapes that resemble corals and sea anemones, which he decorates with fish, sculptures, and shells; he has won many awards for these in flower shows and botanical gardens all over the United States.

Our third stop was to visit a vacant city lot near Moonlight Beach in Encinitas that had been turned into a showcase of amazing succulents and cacti. Dave Dean, who has taken it upon himself to do this, was working in his "garden" when we arrived. He told me the city originally told him that he could not continue with his planting. Part of the allure for all the people who walked by to the beach was that they could admire and walk through his "garden," and he supplied a rock, paint, and a paintbrush so that each person could paint their own rock. Not only did the city acquiesce, but, in 2020, they built a beautiful retaining wall along the sidewalk that borders his garden. On a recent trip to walk through his well-kept-up garden (he spends his weekends weeding, raking the walking paths, planting, and chatting with the many visitors who enjoy the rocks he has installed and sit and enjoy the serenity and beauty), we were able to catch up with him. It is worth the visit alone to see Dave's Rock Garden in Encinitas, California. Dave says he has rocks representing more than 112 countries and plenty of very personalized and interesting ones as well.

Our fourth stop was at Rancho Soledad Nursery in Rancho Santa Fe, well known for specializing in succulents and cacti. When we arrived, the nurseryman, who was supposed to take us around the many acres in his golf cart, was a few minutes late. When he did come to our car, he apologized, as he said he had been on the phone with a customer from Los Angeles who was coming down that afternoon to pick up her $9,000 plant. My comment was, "Was that a nine with three zeros for one plant?" We were taken around the grounds and saw many succulents which we liked and were surprised at how reasonable the prices were and at the tremendous variety. When we saw a particular aloe we

*Aloe vera known for
healing qualities*

*Agave lophanta,
quadricolor variegate*

Agave Blue Flame

*Aeonium "Zwartkop"
flowering . . . count the bees*

Aeonium 'Sunburst'—
simply beautiful

Aloe cameroni

Jeff Moore's undersea succulent scene

liked, the hard part was deciding which of the sometimes 50 to 200 of the same aloe from which to choose. We filled our SUV with beautiful plants. This was the beginning of a yearlong landscaping job. We didn't have enough to plant the entire bank, so we filled in between with low-water shrubs such as lantana and kangaroo paws. We started with no knowledge of this type of gardening, but the bank turned out to be a real showstopper. The remainder of this chapter will show a sample of some of our plants along with some growing suggestions. Jeff Moore's book *Under the Spell of Succulents* has more complete information. There is also a wealth of information online.

Irrigation System

I prefer in-line tubing spaced one foot apart; there are no individual parts to break or complicated hooking things up. The other alternative is the standard large tubing with holes punched in it, to which is attached emitters or 1/4-inch tubing with emitters on the end. Always check the ground with a moisture meter to be sure it's well watered.

Planting

Before I knew about Power Planters, it was hard work to hand-dig a hole for each individual succulent. In either case, just dig a hole big enough to hold the plant, and place some cactus type mix around it. Try to buy a cactus mix that has either pumice or perlite, both of which help aerate the soil and prevent soggy soil and drowned roots. Pumice is best because it is a natural product that has micropores and doesn't float to the surface as perlite tends to, causing the soil to be more compacted and less porous. Perlite is a man-made product and is usually cheaper.

Dave's Rock Garden near Moonlight Beach, Encinitas, California

Fantastic rocks and succulents at Dave's Rock Garden

Dave Dean tending to his creation near Moonlight Beach

CHAPTER 24

Pollination

Pollination is the transfer of plant pollen from the male part of the flower to the female part of the flower, which enables fertilization. It usually occurs by animals such as bats and birds, but mostly by a host of insects such as moths, flies, butterflies, and bees (about 80 percent of all pollination) and wind or water (about 20 percent). Done by hand by humans in backyard gardening and agricultural production, it can enhance fruit production considerably by increasing yield and quality. Quite often, insects and wind are not available. It's not as if we can just make a phone call or dress up like a bee and make it all happen. Besides, it's fun to experience what your handiwork can do. But be careful what you ask for, as it may turn out really weird. For example, if squash and pumpkins are planted close together and they are cross-pollinated, you will not end up with a "squakin." Then again, you might, so it's important to know your species, but, for the purposes of this chapter, I wish to keep it simple. The following three examples pretty much cover how all this works.

Hand Pollination (Helping Out Mother Nature)

CORN

Cut off a tassel, which is the male portion of the plant, consisting of the many "branches" at the top, with small extensions hanging downwards, which contain the pollen. Shake this branch over the top of the silk as it emerges from the corn cob. The silk is the female part, and each silk is a miniature tube that leads to its own individual kernel of corn. The pollen can also be collected in a folded newspaper by shaking the entire tassel and pollen over the newspaper. The pollen is then poured over the silk.

TOMATOES

Each tomato flower is both male and female, and the pollen is transferred from the male stamen to the female pistil within the flower. I usually do this by shaking the entire bush, but I've heard that some gardeners have been using electric toothbrushes to vibrate the tomato flower to help with pollination. "Toothpaste not recommended."

CUCUMBERS

Most vegetables in the cucumber family have separate male and female flowers on the same plant. Each flower opens for one day only. You will need to identify the male and female flowers. The male flowers have a long, thin straight stem and no bulge behind the flower. The female flowers are short and have a small bulge, which is the ovary behind the flower. Male flowers form several days ahead of the females. In the morning, when the male flower first opens, pick it, and remove the petals. This will uncover the stamen containing yellow pollen. Swish the stamen around inside a newly opened female flower; you can use the same stamen for two or three female flowers. Congratulations! You are now a proud papa.

By planting flowering plants that attract hummingbirds, bees, butterflies, and moths, you can increase your chances for natural pollination considerably and can enjoy the beautiful flowers and animals they attract.

CHAPTER 25

Solar, Our Sustainable Future

You may be wondering why I am writing about solar energy in a book on gardening. After recently installing solar-energy panels on our home with no upfront costs to us, and reaping the benefits in our reduced energy bills, I felt compelled to share this. I feel that growing food in your own backyard *and* solar energy are both key components of sustainability. Our solar-energy salesperson told me about the following a few months ago. His company is the second largest of its kind in the United States, with more than 200,000 customers. He also said that solar panels will be a required feature on new houses in California after the state's Building Standards Commission gives final approval to a housing rule that's the first of its kind in the United States. It was set to take effect in 2020, and the new standard includes an exemption for houses that are often shaded from the sun.

When you read the part about Power Purchase Agreements (PPA) in the next section and why this allows everyone who owns a house but does not own panels outright to have a solar system, I think you might be excited about the possibility of solar energy in your own home. This includes businesses and office buildings.

For years, we had wanted to put solar panels on our roof but just kept putting it off due to the perceived costs. We did not know about the Power Purchase Agreement (PPA) offered by several of the solar companies. We were new to the neighborhood, and many of our neighbors had utilized the PPA program, but we assumed they'd purchased their panels outright. A neighbor referred the solar sales rep to us, and this is how he explained the PPA. There are no upfront costs or purchase costs, taxes, leases, or liens, installation costs, or insurance costs, and there is a twenty-year warranty. They market several solar-system options, including outright purchase with cash or buy-on-time-lease arrangements and the very popular PPAs. The PPA has really taken off, much of it due to the fact that so many people are reluctant to invest $20,000 or more in the absence of the above-mentioned benefits. The PPA is an agreement between the solar company and their customer. The way they make money is by providing power through the solar-energy system at a lower rate than the local utility, which results in a lower power bill. They make their money through the power bill over time. They are able to do this because they don't have the costs of transmission lines and infrastructure, as mentioned. You are charged only for the power that the panels on your roof produce. The customer buys the power at a predetermined low rate per kilowatt, with a ceiling rate of no more than 2.9% (this is for our company) a year. Historically, our rates have risen about seven percent annually. The customer still pays them for gas but pays for electric only if they use more than the solar produces in a year. The customer has their own solar-company website, which keeps track of everything. The only thing we pay for is gas, a minimum connection fee, and any extra power we use beyond the total solar system's annual production, which is settled in what they call a True Up fee at the end of a year.

The utility company sends a monthly gas bill and a monthly electric statement (the part that you don't pay) of your date net reading. Our solar company sends us a monthly solar electric statement, which we pay online, for the kilowatts produced by our solar system. To buy the solar system outright would have been $20,000 plus $3000 for an electrician to update our very old and out-of-code circuit-breaker box, thus saving us $23,000 up front. They agreed to do all of this as part of the deal, and they did a beautiful job. A friend saw our system and purchased his own system outright on time because he wanted the state-offered rebate. The salesperson told me that seventy percent of their customers choose the PPA, twenty-nine percent buy on time, and one percent pay cash. Our solar company offers a very nice money incentive for referrals. Please look at my website for up-to-date information, and leave your name and email if you are interested in our solar companies' programs.

Solar panels are constantly evolving, and my hope would be that they will continue to improve in terms of recycling. Global warming and climate change are one of the big topics these days. Our website, digdiego.com, has become one of the go-to places for up-to-date information on the latest legislation and events locally and nationally. It is easy not to keep up. For example, our stove is natural gas, as is our furnace, dryer, and water heater. All but the water heater are ten or more years old, which means we will most likely be looking at repairs or replacements soon. The latest legislation, already passed or in the planning stages, is to eliminate natural gas ASAP. It would be better for us to consider replacing gas appliances—at least one by one. Some of the new technology involves heat pumps and other electrical systems which are much more efficient and cost effective.

Solar-energy systems can be added to your home and come in the following packages and at different prices.

1. Buy a complete system for, say, $20,000 cash. If you stay hooked up to your local grid, they will supply and charge you for any needed extra electricity. Through a system called net metering, you can get credit for any extra electricity your panels produce, In California, the tax rebate is twenty-six percent for 2021.

2. Same as 1), but you have a generator-and-battery backup, which can have an optional hookup to the grid.

3. Same as 1) and 2), except you make a down payment, say $5000, and pay off the remaining balance over ten to twenty years. You can work the numbers so that your monthly payments are the same as your previous electrical bill.

4. The information for this is explained above

We used the PPA without fully understanding all the above options. We went by what five different friends told us and that we would be saving fifty percent or more and would be very happy. If we were younger, we would certainly consider the other options. Be sure you know the pros and cons and options if and when you sell your house. This information should help you to ask the right questions and to be comfortable with your sales rep.

Additional advice: Be sure to do your own research on the following.

1. My stated seven percent rate increase per year may not be accurate. It may be more or may be less. Rates are in such a state of flux, including different rates at different hours of the day in different areas, which makes it difficult to accurately predict solar savings. Our PPA does not save us what we had hoped for, but, overall, we have had nothing but good luck, and we would certainly do it again.

2. Be sure to get a hard, written copy of your contract (not just online), and read it carefully. Sign electronically only if you are comfortable with doing that.

3. Even if you are told there is no lien on your house, there could be a lien on the solar energy system that could affect future property sales or transactions. Be sure to check this point and be comfortable in what you do.

4. If acquiring the solar energy system, a credit check is needed: be sure to know how the check will be done and how often and how it might affect your future financial transactions.

CHAPTER 26

We Are What We Eat

The Indigenous Life and Diet

A s the old saying goes, "We are what we eat—physically, mentally and spiritually."

The Okinawa Study

A University of Hawaii study showed that people living on the island of Okinawa, Japan, have the highest ratio of centenarians and that many have small gardens into old age. In Okinawa, they say that anybody who grows old healthfully needs an *ikigai*, or reason for living. Gardening gives you something to get up for every day. Okinawans also share *yuimaru*, which means a high level of social connectedness. These people gather at local markets and share their garden produce in a large social gathering.

Some studies of elderly people with dementia and Alzheimer's show that they benefit from garden settings, sunlight, and fresh air. This also helps agitated elders feel calmer; plus the colors and textures of plants and vegetables improve tactile and visual ability.

A Harvard University study found that people live longer when surrounded by greenery and have a lower chance of developing cancer or respiratory problems. Small gardens offer physical and mental activity and social get-togethers, so grab your garden gloves and your clippers, and get gardening.

Life Expectancies and Indigenous Cultures

The global population is predicted to be nine billion by 2050, but some experts feel that the planet, unless present food supply and distribution and many other problems are dealt with, will support only five billion.

Cooking and consuming indigenous food means existing in a symbiotic state with our community and environment: to produce just enough, without incurring damage to the people and wildlife around us. The nomadic hunter-gatherers, fishers, and caribou-eating natives of northern Canada vary considerably but have much in common. The same holds true for the aborigines of Australia and natives of Africa. They have learned the secrets of good health through thousands of years of trial and error. They have learned to use whole foods instead of breaking them down into starch, sugars, fats, oils, and protein, and recombining them to look like the natural foods they are not.

For example, you can buy tomato soup, (which may or may not have tomatoes in it), and this may lead you to believe you are eating tomatoes. Processed foods can make it impossible to judge their quality and can be made up of a combination of ingredients of the original food. Modern high-tech food is not alive, because it does not store well. Deterioration can be compensated for by freezing, cooking, or adding chemicals, which slow the growth of bacteria, which themselves are antioxidants. Milk is another example. Pasteurization at high temperatures keeps it from souring, killing the lactobacilli, which are needed for proper digestion.

The list goes on and on, including white bread with the bran and germ being extracted from wheat, which contain many important nutrients.

For ninety-nine percent of our time on Earth, the only thing of importance was determining whether the food was poisonous or not. If not poisonous, we could eat it, and this provided great variety. The variety was dependent on available food and was not the same from season to season. The problem with many modern "convenience" foods is that they lack nutritional quality and many vitamins, minerals, and fiber and have too much sugar, resulting in much obesity.

I have a 523-page book by a dentist, Dr. Weston Price, written many years ago. Although his studies were done in the 1930s, I didn't know about his book until 1980. He has been called "the Isaac Newton of Nutrition." In the 1930s, he traveled around the world, studying the eating habits of various cultures and how they evolved with jaw and tooth development. He found cultures that had less-refined diets had wider jaws than cultures that tended more toward the western diet, which was softer and less nutritious. Their faces were getting smaller and narrower faster than the teeth were getting smaller. These developments were happening rapidly—from one generation to the next.

This kept many of us dentists busy removing wisdom teeth (third molars) and performing orthodontics. I spent two years as a dentist working in the Army Language School and Navy Postgraduate School in the Monterey, California, area. At the time, the language school had instructors or students from many different countries. Looking back, I was able to see these changes across a wide spectrum of humanity. Our dental practice, typical of most dental offices in San Diego, had a large variety of different cultures of patients and employees. I practiced with my father for the first fourteen years and with our older son, Grey, the last fourteen years. After several years, we would accumulate entire families, encompassing four generations, and it was easy to see the changes that Dr. Price had written about in the 1930s. In addition, our patients were developing more dental and medical problems going down the line of generations.

In my own situation, I can cover five generations with similar results. My father should have had orthodontics but didn't have that advantage. I should have but was stubborn and refused. I was fortunate to have my wisdom teeth extracted, which avoided severe problems. Three of our four children all had their wisdom teeth removed and did require orthodontics. Almost all of our fourteen grandchildren (triplets included) had or will have orthodontics. Our great granddaughter, who is eight years old, will have orthodontics in a few years.

Dr. Price did not write much about longevity, but he did write about the increase in health problems when indigenous people were exposed to the western diet. I found it very interesting that one of his studies was of a very remote indigenous community in Switzerland. Looking at life expectancy of the world population of 191 different countries, Japan was number two (both sexes at eighty-five years). Switzerland was number four at eighty-four years, and the United States was number forty-eight at seventy-nine years (data from 2020). It seems that some indigenous cultures, even though they seem to be doing everything right, don't have longevity, probably due to the many variables such as climate change and deforestation.

CHAPTER 27

Grafting and Budding

Grafting goes back four thousand years, to China. Grafting consists of combining together a root stock and a cutting called a "scion." The scion will have the flowers and the fruit, and will be an exact clone of the tree from which it came. In other words, if you have a Fuji apple and cut off the trunk at eighteen inches and graft a Honey Crisp to the trunk, the new tree now bears Honey Crisp and not Fuji apples. The Honey Crisp fruit and leaves feed the roots below through photosynthesis, and the roots supply the fruit and leaves with water and nutrients.

Budding, as opposed to grafting, is relatively new. You end up with a similar result, but a bud is taken from one plant and grown on another. The aspect of grafting and budding I like the most is that it speeds up the propagation process. If I plant an apple or some other tree seed, it will often take five to ten years to mature, and it may not even bear fruit—or, if it does, it may be in a different variety. With grafting and budding, you will get exactly what you want and usually within one to three years.

When we bought our present, much-smaller house, it had a fig tree, which, as closely as we can tell, was about forty years old and produced terrible-tasting fruit. When I say "fruit," I'm not being precise, because a fig is neither a fruit nor a vegetable. It is actually a flower turned inside out. Our friend Scott Jones has his own company, called Plants Comprehensive. He knows so much about plants that I kid him about having a PhD in "plantology." He came over and cut the fig tree off three feet above the ground, which left an eighteen-inch-wide base that divided into three different eight-inch-wide branches. I had collected scions (six-inch pieces) from three different types of figs trees—Black Mission, Taste of Honey, and Azore (Portuguese). Scott grafted the first stump with the Azore variety and showed me how easy it was to graft. I was able to finish the last of the other two varieties on the remaining two stumps myself. This particular type of grafting is called bark grafting. Each variety ripens in successive order and has two crops. In the second year, we had lots of figs; the season lasts from June through November.

When to Graft

Budding can be done before or during the growing season, but grafting is usually done in the winter or early spring, when the scions and root stocks are dormant.

How to Select Scion Wood

Use clean, sharp shears or knives that have been sterilized by dipping in isopropyl alcohol or a mixture of one part of household bleach with nine parts of water. It's best to use the scion the same day that it is cut, but it can also be stored in a Ziplock bag in the refrigerator for a month or so.

Types of Grafts

Cleft graft—Very simple and quite popular, and can be done on main stems or on lateral branches. The root stock should be one to four inches in diameter. The scion should be about 1/4 inch in diameter, usually about six inches long—but long enough to have at least three buds. Preparation of the root stock involves sawing it off cleanly and using a cleft tool wedge or a chisel with a mallet or hammer to drive the tool through the center of the stock down two or three inches. Hold the cleft open with the chisel or the pick end of the clefting tool. Select two scions, and, with a grafting or new utility knife, make a cut starting at the base of the lowest bud on each scion, and make two opposing tapered cuts, about two inches long, toward its base. The side with the lowest bud should be a little thicker than the opposing side. Insert the scion on each side of the cleft with the wider side of the wedge facing outward. The cambium layer (which lies between the bark and the inner wood) of the scion needs to contact the cambium of the root stock. Remove the clefting tool, and the cleft will close on the scions. Seal everything well with grafting goop to prevent drying. When the first growing season is finished, prune off the weaker of the two scions.

Bark Graft—This is usually used with a root stock of four to twelve inches in diameter. Do this in early spring, so that the bark slips easily from the wood but before any major sap flow. Cut off the root stock cleanly. Make a vertical slit two inches long through the bark. I like to put no more than four scions on each root stock. Cut the base of each scion to a two-inch tapered wedge on one side only. Loosen the bark, and insert the scion so that the tapered side is against the exposed wood. Drive a small brad or nail through the bark and the scion into the root stock. Seal everything well with grafting goop.

Side Veneer Graft—With this graft, you can add a scion without cutting off the main part of the tree, which can be done later. These are usually done on young seedlings and not mature trees. By not cutting off the entire top, if the graft fails, the graft area will heal, and you can graft again. The diameter of the scion should be closer to the root stock, if possible. Again, use an approximately six-inch scion, and it can be grafted to a larger root stock. Cut downwards on the side of the root stock, and separate a one- to two-inch-long flap veneer containing the bark cambium. Make the scion match the bare spot on the root stock by cutting down one side of the scion. Hold the scion, and cut another angled piece off the other side to fit the peeled piece of root stock. Match the root stock and scion together, wrap some parafilm tightly around the entire graft, and be sure the cambium of the scion and root stock line up; cover everything with a grafting compound or grafting paint so that it doesn't dry out.

If the graft is good, it should start growing within two or three weeks.

Splice Graft—This is a fairly simple graft, joining a scion to a root stock, both of which should be the same diameter and about 1/2 inch or less. Cut the root stock off on a diagonal, one-inch cut, and make a similar cut on the base of the scion. Place the scion on the root stock, and wrap it with parafilm, followed by grafting compound or grafting paint.

Budding

Budding, instead of using a scion, is a technique in which a single bud is utilized. This can be done just before or during the growing season. Some species may be budded during the winter, while dormant. This type of graft is quite often used for citrus. Cut off a dormant bud with a single slice, and cut a "T" into the bark of your root stock. Start the scion cut 1/2 inch below the bud; cut upwards just under the bark to 1/4 to 1/2 inch above the bud. Make a second horizontal cut above the bud, deep enough so that the bud and bark and a thin sliver of wood come with it. Place the bud in the "T," being sure that it is in good contact with the root stock. Wrap it with parafilm, and coat it with grafting goop or paint.

More Ideas on Grafting

These grafting techniques will suffice for most situations, but if you want to go further, there are many more methods available on the Internet. Be sure to use scions and buds that are compatible with the root stock; this information can also be found online. For example, if you are grafting apples to apples and peaches to peaches, it's all pretty straightforward, but if you want to have some real fun, you will be able to graft many different varieties, some of which will be successful, and some of which won't. So have fun, and get grafting.

CHAPTER 28

A Wonderful Hike

To spice things up, I wish to cover some very old but interesting technology. A few years ago, I was hiking with our daughter and some friends in our local mountains. We sat down to have lunch on a large granite boulder under what has to be the largest oak tree of all time. Its diameter was about fifteen feet and circumference about thirty feet, with its canopy of branches extending about one hundred feet in diameter. I learned later that these trees can live for up to 600 years.

At this point, I wish to toss in some information about seed size, which varies considerably. If you have ever had the opportunity to see a carrot seed, you know that they are so tiny that some of them are sold in pellets so they can be more easily planted. To put this into perspective, consider the following: a seed for some orchids is the size of a grain of sugar, which is awfully small for containing all the DNA and other information it needs to determine weather patterns and water availability and when to sprout, etc.

Acorn grinding holes made by Native Americans, San Diego County

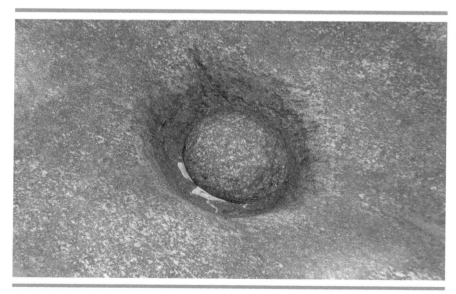

Metate with granite grinding rock

On the other side of the coin is a huge seed, up to fifty pounds, that grows a special palm tree only on two islands in the south seas. Lying somewhere in between are acorns, which average about one inch long but grow these huge oak trees. What is interesting about these acorns is that they provide food for deer, squirrels, and all sorts of wild creatures. Our local Native Americans ground up acorns in large quantities hundreds of years ago and used them for a food source. The grinding was done by a round stone in a hole in granite rock called a metate (our modern version would be mortar and pestle).

Back to sitting on the boulder while eating our lunch: My friend Joe Barry asked me to move my leg, as he thought I might be sitting on something interesting, which I was. I had seen quite a few metates through the years, but the grinding stones were long gone. After I brushed aside the oak leaves, I discovered not only a metate but the grinding stone perfectly polished and sized for the hole—a rare find. Upon further investigation, we found several more metates holding their grinding stones. Long story short: After much hoopla and taking a few photos, we covered our miraculous finds with lots of oak leaves in hopes they would go undiscovered for another few hundred years.

Acknowledgments

This book was a family project. I would dictate from notes and rough outlines to my wife Joan, who would type (she started typing my term papers when she was in the 7th grade) and suggest corrections. From there the chapter would be emailed to the real gardener in the family, our eldest daughter Jeri, to refine and send it back for us to review. Sometimes she would send it to our youngest son, John, who teaches at Baylor University in Texas and has written several textbooks and screenplays. He would edit further and add his special humor. Our oldest son, Grey, a dentist with a good sense of humor, added a lot of great ideas. Our youngest daughter, Tracy, was very busy during all this trying to keep her six children, including teenage triplets, under control. All this took one year, and we were finally able to combine everything, including photos, and send it all to 1106 Design for professional design and editing. My heartfelt thanks to everyone who helped me, including Jeri and Elizabeth Pessemier for the wonderful pictures they took.

I am very fortunate to have had wonderful parents and in-laws who were so nice and generous over the years. Our good friend A. Lee Brown had just finished ten years writing his novel *The Varsity* (foreword by Tom Brokaw) when I started writing this book. I have a folder full of email answers from him to my many questions. He is a professor with two PhDs who loves to teach and is very generous with his time and advice; I'm very grateful to him. A big thank you to Jeff Moore of Solana Succulents for allowing me to use some of his beautiful succulent photos. Greg Neiwold was very helpful in getting me started with several of his Power Planters. Dave Dean's beautiful rock and succulent garden in Encinitas inspired me to plant my own succulents.

Lastly, I am very grateful for my parents being organic farmers, much ahead of their time, and getting me started in gardening.

Resources

BOOKS

Vegetable Gardening for Dummies
Charlie Nardozzi

Sunset Western Garden Book
Sunset Publishing Corporation

California Gardener's Guide
Nan Sterman

Southern California Gardening
Pat Welsh

Worms Eat My Garbage
Mary Appelhof and Joanne Olszewski

The Urban Farmer
Curtis Stone

The Year-Round Vegetable Gardener
Niki Jabbour

Let It Rot
Stu Campbell

Dead Snails Leave No Trails
Loren Nancarrow and Janet Hogan Taylor

Free Plants for Everyone
David The Good

The Pruner's Bible
Steve Bradley

Four-Season Harvest
Eliot Coleman

Under the Spell of Succulents
Jeff Moore

Aloes & Agaves in Cultivation
Jeff Moore

Grow Your Soil
Diane Miessler

Urban Gardening
Kevin Espiritu

Grow Bag Gardening
Kevin Espiritu

ONLINE SOURCES—MOST ARE .COM

San Diego Seed Company

Renee's Garden Seeds

PowerPlanter

Epic Gardening

Next Level Gardening

Gardeners Supply

Cali Kim Garden and Home

MI Gardener

Gardener Scott

Roots and Refuge

Solana Succulents

Plants Comprehensive

Behlen Country

Index

About the Author

I was born and raised in San Diego and grew up helping my parents in their large organic garden. Fortunately, because of our wonderful Southern California climate, we were able to grow fruits and vegetables year round. I had lots of pets and different hobbies, but the "seed" was definitely planted in my mind about the benefits and pleasures of gardening. Little did I know that 80 years later it would still hold the same fascination. After high school and dental school at USC, I worked on patients at the Army Language School and Navy Postgraduate School in the Monterey area for two years. I then returned to San Diego and worked with my father, also a USC dentist, for many years. During this time I married my high school sweetheart and raised four children in the house we built on the same block as my parents. My father would often come over and give me advice and show our children his "how to" knowledge from 51 years of gardening. My book about gardening for 80 years features how growing your own fruits and vegetables can be both productive and fun.

Jon Cunningham's love of gardening shines through in this very practical and information-packed book. This is a must read for the aspiring gardener.

~Lawrence Mulryan

Master Gardener

Former Mayor of San Raphael, California

Former CEO of California State Workman's Compensation Fund

Jon Cunningham's *Around My Garden in Eighty Years* is a wonderful read, not only for master gardeners but all levels of growers. It is well-written and illustrated providing both humor and tips based on a lifetime of growing sustainable fruits, vegetables and succulents. The author's depth of knowledge is obvious by his gifted discussions of soils, water, seeds, and contemporary techniques.

~A. Lee Brown Jr., Ph.D.

Professor *emeritus*

Author of *The Varsity, A Story of America's Underage Warriors in WWll*

I hope you enjoyed this book.
Would you do me a favor?

Like all authors, I rely on online reviews to encourage future sales. Your opinion is invaluable. Would you take a few moments now to share your assessment of my book on Amazon or any other book-review website you prefer? Your opinion will help the book marketplace become more transparent and useful to all. Thank you very much!